How To Find All Missing Persons / Unsolved Cases. And Collect All Reward Offers. Volume XXVIII. THE CASE OF MELISSA HUNT

DAVID GOMADZA

www.twofuture.world

Copyright © 2024 David Gomadza

All rights reserved.

Paperback **ISBN:** 9798327938519

DEDICATION

To a better future.

CONTENTS

How To Find All Missing Persons /
Unsolved Cases.
And Collect All Reward Offers. Volume XXVIII
THE CASE OF MELLISA HUNT   1

The Afterlife Conversation

and The Council Of Creation.   7

The Killers.   15

ACKNOWLEDGMENTS

Tomorrow's World Order

How To Find All Missing Persons / Unsolved Cases. And Collect All Reward Offers. Volume XXVIII. THE CASE OF MELLISA HUNT

BACKGROUND INFORMATION

The NSW Government, together with the NSW Police Force, has announced a $1 million reward for information into the murder of Hunter woman, Melissa Hunt, more than 26 years ago.

The body of Melissa Hunt, then aged 22, was found near the weir wall of Burrenjim Dam, Bluegum Creek via Stockrington, on Monday 25 April 1994.

A post mortem examination revealed she died from severe head injuries.

Strike Force Impey, comprised of detectives from the Lake Macquarie Police District and the State Crime Command's Homicide Squad, was formed to investigate her death; however, no arrests have been made.

How To Find All Missing Persons / Unsolved Cases. And Collect All Reward Offers.
Volume XXVIII. THE CASE OF MELISSA HUNT

Following a Coronial Inquest in 1998, the matter was sent to the Office of the Director of Public Prosecutions for review and referred to the Unsolved Homicide Unit.

A formal review of the investigation was conducted under the new unsolved framework and is now under re-investigation by detectives attached to Strike Force Circulo.

As inquiries continue, police are renewing their appeal to the community to come forward with any information that may assist detectives with their investigation.

Minister for Police and Emergency Services, David Elliott, said he hopes the $1 million NSW Government incentive will bring detectives a step closer to finding answers for Melissa's family.

"The NSW Government pledges a $1 million reward in the hope that it will assist police in their efforts to get to the bottom of this horrific crime, and that it will go some way in delivering justice for Melissa and her family," Mr Elliott said.

"The community will not, and should not, forget the tragic circumstances surrounding Melissa's disappearance almost three decades ago. I urge anyone with even the seemingly smallest piece of information to come forward."

Homicide Squad Commander, Detective Superintendent Danny Doherty, said Strike Force Circulo investigators have conducted a thorough review of the case to explore all possible lines of inquiry.

"In October this year, officers returned to the Burrenjim Dam with specialist police from the Forensic Evidence and Technical Services Command to conduct a full review of the original crime scene," Det Supt Doherty said.

How To Find All Missing Persons / Unsolved Cases. And Collect All Reward Offers. Volume XXVIII. THE CASE OF MELISSA HUNT

"Items of interest that were recovered during initial inquiries have also undergone further forensic testing, to ensure every avenue of investigation is identified and pursued.

"Detectives have also been liaising with interstate law enforcement partners as we believe there are associates and witnesses residing in other states – including Queensland, Victoria and South Australia – that are yet to come forward and speak with police.

"As inquiries into Melissa's death continue, detectives are urging anyone with information to contact police so we may provide much-needed answers and closure for Melissa's family," Det Supt Doherty said.

Melissa's brother, Mr Peter Hallett, said he hoped the reward may help detectives uncover new leads to finally provide justice for his sister and family.

"Melissa was deeply loved by our family and we have never stopped missing her and desperately wishing that her life had not been cut short," Mr Hallett said mischievous laugh, musical talent, eye for detail, passion for writing and fierce love for her family and two children – we should all be able to hold her now.

"After 26 years of despairing grief, we are hoping that someone will come forward and help police identify those responsible for her death.

"Melissa was robbed of her life and of her right to know and love her children, and as a family we cannot rest until justice is served," Mr Hallett said.

Anyone with information that may assist Strike Force Circulo

How To Find All Missing Persons / Unsolved Cases. And Collect All Reward Offers.
Volume XXVIII. THE CASE OF MELISSA HUNT

detectives is urged to contact Crime Stoppers: 1800 333 000 or https://nsw.crimestoppers.com.au. Information is treated in strict confidence. The public is reminded not to report crime via NSW Police social media pages

TOMORROW'S WORLD ORDER'S PERSPECTIVES

USE OF PREDEFINED AFTERLIFE PARAMETERS

These guide souls the moment it exist the human body on its journey to Yahweh the creator these define what to do and what to expect as you go to hell or heaven if a souk leaves earth it enters ozone orbit and instantly everything reboots for it to start a new phase of life after living the earth's body now what happens is that it enters the ozone orbit and a simply click caused by the sudden drop of pressure from -1186 to – 20 means the bottom shaft of the soul will lift rapidly and this pushes its back into the air higher than its head best example is a penguin but with real human legs and head just the shape now God created a life predefined program for them instead of asking what should I do and where should I go they instantly know from predefined stencils if you did well and talked most about God then heaven is for you if you did evil and talked more about the devil then the devil is yours now if we Ask what can be of humans without souks this is the answer dead forever your soul is you a new transformation to the electromagnetic waves life where you see Yahweh for the first time and praise him and wish you had seen him a long time ago because of his Majesty and will always be there forever now what are all these you may ask these are rules to be guided by in the creation court in short it has everything humans know about the judges and the presiding judge who will always be Yahweh and 84 angels surrounding the altar 28 high priests who always say Yahweh have mercy on humans and 74 smaller courts priests who always say Yahweh has mercy on humans and 96 princesses who say glory to Yahweh forever and ever amen we have 96 elders who always say if I can why he can't meaning if the devil can drink blood why can't Yahweh who created the devil and blood do the same now this is not the same as saying if the devil can kill why can Yahweh its more on professional grounds rather than challenging now if we look at the inside of the court we have 81 priests surrounding the altar who say Yahweh be merciful to humans but if they disobey you we put hem on trial for you and kill them for you almighty Yahweh inside this is a round circle where Yahweh sits

How To Find All Missing Persons / Unsolved Cases. And Collect All Reward Offers. Volume XXVIII. THE CASE OF MELISSA HUNT

and asks questions now if we look deep inside the court you will see that there are other things that resemble earth high courts like benches and chairs 10 times human sizes for the gods who are so enormous 2 are equal to 84 billion humans in size
predefined parameters for humans after death as in know what is inside is a large size of books the book of creation is among them with 108978678928367890123486789012458617890 11 pages and is divided into humans first then chapter for animals then a chapter for angles then a chapter for gods and a chapter for Joseph Yahweh's best friend and a chapter for Yahweh's best friend's wife Anna and a chapter for Yahweh's wife Catitighit and lastly a chapter for Yahweh and recently a chapter for davidgomadza as Yahweh's representative on earth marking the new beginnings starting in 2025

1. tell us who killed you
2. tell us what killed you
3. tell us why and who killed you
4. tell us why you died
5. tell us what could have been done and is not done
6. tell us what could be and why
7. tell is when this happened
8. tell us why this is so
9. tell us why this is so
10. what can be done to improve this

What does the book of creation say about davidgomadza David Gomadza is the first and last ruler to be appointed by Yahweh fir the next 25 billion years and will act as his representative on earth deciding cases and upholding his principles on earth and as such has been entitled to 489 trillion dollars in assets this number signifies eternity among humans and the beginning of a new Era chapter 7867892802893862841890287689018320867890123486789018236 487289128610 Creation manual the new Era of new electromagnetic wave conduit signed and dated by Yahweh himself on 27may2024 at 237800 Yatime
creation.universe.ya.start.end.find.davidgomadza.ya.askya.ya

Ask.read.creation.manucreation.universe.ya.start.end.find.davidgoma

How To Find All Missing Persons / Unsolved Cases. And Collect All Reward Offers.
Volume XXVIII. THE CASE OF MELISSA HUNT

askya.ya

Ask.rulesofthecourt.start.now.start
David Gomadza welcome the rules of court are guiding principles that tell you what to do and how to do it first you must always say I believe in the court of creation and I shall abide by he rules of this court and shall always do things according to the rules of this court in deciding the cases I am assigned to you must ask what can be done so that you know all your options before making choices the court system will make it easy to check files and ask the outcomes of the decision ask the court the final decision in any case.

THE AFTERLIFE CONVERSATION AND THE COUNCIL OF CREATION'S ANAYLSIS.

melissa hunt she died of severe headaches injuries in an accident at asert devon county in queensland after challenging a man called artop athen who said if you challenge then you can get everything you want but silently on hell then put down his hand and said the challenge is for you to say i can if he can then to go to the next challenge that is ask what can be done then go to the next challenge then ask what has been done then go to the next challenge and say what is to be done after that then you finish but at this point it will be so dark to see that you can only lose or die of falling hard on rocks she agreed on the belief that when she doesn't want then it will be easy because she can easily stop and go home then she started very well that 3 other people who were there thought that she can finish then she said after this round i will do one last one no matter the outcome i will go home but this man remained quiet because at this point the rules allowed her safe passage home then she started and instantly fell deep down in a ravine and something inside screamed so hard and jumped out and flew to the sky still screaming i run she died long ago 8 seconds deep down ventilation is bad and escaped to the skies still screaming then the man first looked alarmed and said how she dropped down just after the best round and asked the others who didn't understand anything after he said i got 33 counts then all

How To Find All Missing Persons / Unsolved Cases. And Collect All Reward Offers. Volume XXVIII. THE CASE OF MELISSA HUNT

remained silent until shout 3 seconds then he repeated again the count and said i lost one round to her let's start another round without her but this time one said 32 i count not and he opened his eyes but he didn't not say anything but looked at the man and said she fell oh god so deep how did this happen surely i had not thought she could fall so fast this was to be the easiest round then he said she come to impress us but simply dropped we can continue next and he got up and ran down the gorge to look for her shouting her name saying mellisa melissa but when he arrived she was dead he touch her wrist to check pulse and said she truly died and ran away fast his name is atorp mnop real name adeva aterst who said what can be said of women who only fuck after winning but then when they win they ran away then come and fuck the next day though now as he was running the man shouted at the most top of his voice and said if you run then you pushed her so he stopped and he said i don't run then who is to be fucked at the end the only vagina died and is now cold now if you ask what this means is that one of the guys can take her place but they all refused to stand for her then he said
melissa hunt who was killed by aropt astovern who said do you want to play a game of death but you must be willing to die if not don't try at all and she agreed thinking it's a test of courage then on the 6th round she fell in the pit and instantly died that her soul escaped at 2 seconds out of the 8 long ago seconds it gave her and the time it was over she was already dead but when one of them checked her the other main one said come and play or else then it's you who killed her otherwise why do you run and he returned his name was asterp who said ok and started playing resulting in a deliberate fall to escape but the other two started a manhunt until he fell to his dead leaving just two persons who continued until the man who arranged the game fell deliberately to make him jump from a higher position then he realised that the best is to jump on him but he rolled to the side and everyone died leaving him then he had sex with the dead woman and took her inside as all this was in his yard for days he had sex with her body then said if i can then they can so i will leave the body but clean it up of any fluids and leave it there for someone else to find her but none of those who saw her wanted anything top do with her she had head injuries that were so bad that if you look at her

How To Find All Missing Persons / Unsolved Cases. And Collect All Reward Offers.
Volume XXVIII. THE CASE OF MELISSA HUNT

you could not believe that she was a real person then he said if none want anything to do with her then what and took her and had more sex with her and said today i will send you like that maybe someone gets interested and when a young man saw vagina then he said oh my god she is a real human why no one take notice now i can see vagina and for that oh it has sperm in it if i add mine then i can call the police and tell them then he knelt but another passerby said you go to jail for adding because you protect the real killer so he stop and wanked instead and ran away so that his sperm is as far possible and he called the police and said a smelly decomposing body is outside why you can't remove it did you order its killing then a police van arrived and took the body and closed the whole area including where he dropped his sperm and left he came back and took the sand and went then another night he returned and set the place on fire after reading that sniffer dogs can smell sperm then he called again and said i called you when i found the body so who killed her did you find this son of a bitch who kill a beautiful woman like that or i look for him myself since i know how his sperm smells and the police said how you smelled the sperm reports say she was cleaned but you talk about sperm and he said don't fuck up with me you covering for the killer why and he said i didn't know there was sperm but we can check again he is pc atoop who said what if another decides to kill and blame everyone else but himself then what and laughed and said that would be hilarious because everyone else will be locked for his crime giving us work but then a knock at the door and sergent artogfg said who he day dream about killings in this county is made and deserve to be killed by everyone else but who have guts to die at the hands of the people before we even looked at the case then knowingly put this aside as unsolved but get the killer removed somehow to remove the risk but spend hours and getting paid putting everything together but non to know but god only then he said lord i am ready and put a gun to himself and pretended to shoot himself. said i will go to the priest first and said father forgive me for i have sinned but one person must die by my hand and said can i but and sat down just before the priest came and said have we sinned haven't we and silenced then he said it wasn't me i have my own reason to and the father said okay can you tell me what's thus about

How To Find All Missing Persons / Unsolved Cases. And Collect All Reward Offers. Volume XXVIII. THE CASE OF MELISSA HUNT

and he said i am thinking and said that some muggers might die tonight if we find who killed this woman but he said i don't know about this but then he said can i ask what can be of priest who side with muggers and he said i don't mug nor ask muggers to come here but they do and who said a policeman is not a mugger some mug your wife's life for a loaf of bread just to have something to talk about for years or a job to come to but everyone us tge same but if we look at the situation at hand then muggers are better than policemen because muggers mug to eat one day's and skip the next 30 but policemen muggers everyday until they come a honest man like the priest to lie for him god know all your evil acts now what does all this mean it means that the picevv deliberately got a mother killed and be abused then cover up everything with the aim of getting the man killed by the mob so they are asking the priest to lie that he don't know who killed the woman as it turns out that he saw the body and sent message to this police and then expected the police to have come to collect the body then said well did you get my message that there is a body but you ignored my message and now you are here so that i lie about the killing i can't god judges people you harshly and you will burn in hell but he said i am god do you think that there is a god out there who can come and rescue people then he said okay you think this is a game right them we must sit and watch and see if god will come and rescue this woman and there was no help she dropped on the 6th send code [ ] and say sleep forever and now she said what are you doing you should have said there is no god and then she was not going to expect god then you should have said falling kills meaning death kills so she understand then you should have said say stop at 5 and go home now she is dead because people have placed too much reliance on god who never show up why father you pretend to know when you don't know a thing what i expected from you was this for you to tell her that tomorrow don't go or you will die because roastop means death in aboriginal australian language how we teach these kids when they are young is that roastop means death and will never associate himself or herself with roastop she should have said i know you are death that was his ticket that he played a part in all this but you even though she said i trust father i will ask him tomorrow then why you did not show her death so that she is afraid enough to

How To Find All Missing Persons / Unsolved Cases. And Collect All Reward Offers.
Volume XXVIII.   THE CASE OF MELISSA HUNT

run when death nears but the priest now upset said you tricked her there is a reward after what did you say that it was and he said sex as the reward but a day after and he said why sex as a reward to a married woman is that justified and he said it's not working its there but no action so what can she do then he said tell them to work things out nit to take her out of a lovely family these cheap policemen of nowadays literally getting an innocent half wit though woman killed so that they have a job and to make things worse and to ignore all calls for help to remove the body living it there until it started to decompose surely you must have some decency in you your challenging of god is iterate because if he come will start crying because if you ask everyone you had an opportunity to do things right remove the body and get the killer this is what happened the killer took her out look i even took the black and white photos and then sent you the next day surprisingly they were opened recorded given a police evidence number and he picked the up and red the number 879865423180 police department forensic science department mentioned 11 queensland police station dated 29879 now i have to live with this lie that you care about the people or do your job properly we pay your wages this is what people complain about that the government don't pay you the people who you work for refused to pay you and we decided to pay you and now you literally sit down when we agreed to pay the police in the 1976 charter when the government wanted to abolish the police we agreed that we can contribute so that you get paid from our wages a certain percentage and now you same people now come and say things like this to us this can't be accepted unless and he stopped talking and looked at him and said you must be out of your mind who can even ask what happen to to you everyone know there were two other guys with the woman one might have beaten him up exactly he will simply say that she fell down and was an accident but she was aware because rules were explained to her and as such what could i possible do then what then we have to let him go that would not be justice but if you confront him all together surely no matter how strong he is you will get some sense of justice you know why i am saying this things like these are not police matter he is within the law but with a woman that type we call slow that is not fair we must act and make sure that he

How To Find All Missing Persons / Unsolved Cases. And Collect All Reward Offers.
Volume XXVIII. THE CASE OF MELISSA HUNT

pays a price he deserves now if you ask what he did and what the law can do to him then you will see that there is no justice at all justice is to get him killed as well so can you arrange this or not because as far as i know he is badly injured attacked by one of tg1e man if he dies then one of the men killed him case closed and everyone is happy ever wonder who owns a house that big and he doesn't work how does he pay bills and he is never late he pays on time always what does this have to do with the woman now i see what this is all about you want his house but everything else legal means no hands on his house but if we the mob kill him then you get to get the house how much and stopped i don't know what you are talking about then go away right now before i report you to the police commissioner ian tonert he is my cousin and will trust me rather than house thieves mind your words father if i can get a thug killed i can get a priest killed easily so do as i say fir 8% in 5 but 1 since he will be dead and he walked out leaving the priest think then he stopped and said if you do him tonight then it's 10% but tomorrow's might be nothing we move in ourselves that means the house remains his then the priest instantly the priest knelt down and said father forgive me fir i have sinned an innocent woman died and must be revenge i will organise this his real name is father torrs wopqrstuvw meaning staurt who was 72 at the time and who said what can be of thieves that still houses and ask the priest to do their dirty deeds if this is so then what can be of these dirty cops he looked lost and said if he can then we can after this on and he looked in the mirror and said god why people with responsibilities for others neglect their duties only to beg a priest a retire officer to come back and do their work i am 72 years old and what can i do at this age but i will serve justice for the woman and for dirty cops sue them or kill them myself i still have my badge and gun and i can protect the people nit these doggy cops he sat down and took his cap and wore it and left going to a house across the street and said let's go and gathered the mob the boy celebrated and took out a huge knife and said i have waited for this for a long time and he went to the house and when he came out the police had gathered outside after learning that the priest was a police man before this job but just parked their cars and waited for the people to act and he said if they can then we can and clapped hands and run

How To Find All Missing Persons / Unsolved Cases. And Collect All Reward Offers. Volume XXVIII. THE CASE OF MELISSA HUNT

away but a group of people suddenly appeared and said he won't live after this day and asked him to come out of which he did and said how do i pay these crooks said kill the woman the husband gets life insurance she has over 2 million dollars which can help the husband with acert insurance now if he runs then we late him go and take his house but if he refuse then we have to kill him and he said if we can then what can be then they all gathered and said what can be is to be and what was can be and he took out a gun and aimed at pc atorp and killed him then he aimed at pc asetop and killed him then one of then opened fire and killed him then one said what can be said of police who are so crooked they need the mob to be killed then they all laughed and said look how justice works in miraculous ways the crook broke dirty cops and got then killed out easily 2 in seconds which could have taken decades and a lot of our hard earned money now we are in peace and they all celebrated and said today we have seen justice from all sides as such we must celebrate this and ask what can be of cities with law abiding citizens then this is the answer they can be prosperous and witness justice all the time now if we ask what can be justice then it's the killing of the man who killed an innocent half wit woman then do everything write so that when he is arrested his house can be served because he has to give address that remains on the files for ever meaning no house for the police
but justice for everyone all this he did so he walk out in court therefore an accidental verdict was record by the court of creation as the man used all this to protect his house from the thieving police that he took all reasonable steps to get arrested but because he is right their target is not justice but the property he owns such circumstances need a deep analysis because as we now know the woman fell at the best round round 6 because of a code 82678902836789028 that controls motor neurons and she fainted using a code 284 then was dissipated using a dissipate dot humans brain of subject now to hell dot start after this the city changed two new police officers were recruited who loved the locals and one was the former priest who said once a cop always a cop i had killed so many bad guys including cops that if i didn't become a priest i could have gone straight to hell after reception everyone laughed.
therefore the court of creation finds the woman as died of her own

How To Find All Missing Persons / Unsolved Cases. And Collect All Reward Offers. Volume XXVIII. THE CASE OF MELISSA HUNT

ignorance as a normal woman would have run or screamed for help. the end
artop athen / artop astern who said what can be of cops who steal houses under the disguise of murder and hide all evidence and refuse all appeals by the killer to turn himself only to get the house registered as his because his parents died when their car exploded on the highway with all house documents on them on 10 february 1978 one year before mellisa hunt died of severe head injuries at the hands of artop astern who was going to argue that a woman with two kids a husband a house worthy 2 million and a life insurance of same value to the house can never be called half wit because she has achieved the average if not more of any woman out there the reason why the police are calling her half wit is because they do this to lower her self esteem so that she does what they want especially in this case the other two men volunteered because of the chance of sex the next day me all i wanted was money for the mortgage she had promised me if i treated her like a grown up and not like a half wit that made all her children be laughed at at school in the end refusing to go to school and now because of house chores she is so tired that sex with husband is minimal that is she asks him he always make an excuse as it turns put he had already married another woman legally meaning she was literally kicked out of the house guess by who served her with an eviction notice the day before the incident the same policeman who said she is a half wit if we ask the husband why then his answer is this they refused her to sign any papers by sending her a code 28689028498208678092 that says do not open any papers until sergent artop said so yours loved one only thisessage all the time she had deleted as it turns out he had sit with his mother like wife and was wooing her out of a marriage by sending secret messages using government property to protect these women and said can i if you can but ...we can get married at last a real wedding you want but make sure he fall first if you do i lose everything you and gge house so what do you say and she said okay but ...you are still married but the marriage never died because all he wanted was sex with her after she deliberately opened her knickers and showed him her vagina when he called her half wit in front of everyone when she thought he wanted to marry her then forced her into this

relationship by escaping calling this gentlemen he wanted but for nothing just to have a reason to come to the neighborhood and wank in the woods whispering her name then curse after he cum now if we look at this case then the pice man has played a big role to influence her life and what is to be that means if the justice was right he could have been sent to jail his coordinates are 08987638678902849828028468901234861028417809838201480876 2841090236 in south of queensland in a grave marked atorp astern a dedicated police officer father and son you will be missed 08 06 1980
the end

THE KILLER, THE CONFESSIONS AND THE COORDINATES

an accidental verdict was record by the court of creation as the man used all this to protect his house from the thieving police that he took all reasonable steps to get arrested but because he is right their target is not justice but the property he owns such circumstances need a deep analysis because as we now know the woman fell at the best round round 6 because of a code 82678902836789028 that controls motor neurons and she fainted using a code 284 then was dissipated using a dissipate dot humans brain of subject now to hell dot start after this the city changed two new police officers were recruited who loved the locals and one was the former priest who said once a cop always a cop i had killed so many bad guys including cops that if i didn't become a priest i could have gone straight to hell after reception everyone laughed.
therefore the court of creation finds the woman as died of her own ignorance as a normal woman would have run or screamed for help.

artop athen / artop astern who said what can be of cops who steal houses under the disguise of murder and hide all evidence and refuse all appeals by the killer to turn himself only to get the house registered as his because his parents died when their car exploded on the highway with all house documents on them on 10 february 1978 one year before mellisa hunt died of severe head injuries at the hands of artop astern who was going to argue that a woman with two kids a husband a house worthy 2 million and a life insurance of same value to the house can never be called half wit because she has achieved the average if not more of any woman out there the reason why the police are calling her half wit is because they do this to lower her self esteem so that she does what they want especially in this case the other two men volunteered because of the chance of sex the next day me all i wanted was money for the mortgage she had promised me if i treated her like a grown up and not like a half wit

…I found God…visit www.twofuture.world

THE CLAIM

the reward offer

THE COLLECTION

www.twofuture.world/donate

ABOUT DAVID GOMADZA

visit www.twofuture.world

signed david gomadza
ask.davidgomadzaauthorised.licensed.checkya.askya.ya

08 June 2024 12.04 pm
scotland
00447719210295
davidgomadza@hotmail.com
info@twofuture.world

How To Find All Missing Persons / Unsolved Cases. And Collect All Reward Offers.
Volume XXVIII. THE CASE OF MELISSA HUNT

www.ingramcontent.com/pod-product-compliance
Lightning Source LLC
Chambersburg PA
CBHW031518210526
45464CB00007B/2976